Contents

Being fair means thinking of
other people.

Citizenship

Being Fair

Cassie Mayer

www.heinemann.co.uk/library
Visit our website to find out more information about Heinemann Library books.

To order:
 Phone 44 (0) 1865 888066
Send a fax to 44 (0) 1865 314091
Visit the Heinemann Bookshop at www.heinemann.co.uk/library to browse our catalogue and order online.

First published in Great Britain by Heinemann Library,
Halley Court, Jordan Hill, Oxford OX2 8EJ, part of Harcourt
Education. Heinemann is a registered trademark of Harcourt
Education Ltd.

Editorial: Cassie Mayer and Charlotte Guillain
Design: Joanna Hinton-Malivoire
Illustrated by Mark Beech
Art editor: Ruth Blair
Production: Duncan Gilbert

Printed and bound in China by South China
Printing Co. Ltd.

ISBN 978 0 431 18674 0 (hardback)
11 10 09 08 07
10 9 8 7 6 5 4 3 2 1

ISBN 978 0 431 186825 (paperback)
12 11 10 09 08
10 9 8 7 6 5 4 3 2 1

British Library Cataloguing in Publication Data
Mayer, Cassie
Being fair. - (Citizenship)
1. Fairness - Juvenile literature
I. Title
177.7
A full catalogue record for this book is available from the
British Library

Being fair means treating people well.

When you share your toys …

you are being fair.

When you wait your turn ...

you are being fair.

When you give someone else
a turn ...

you are being fair.

When you share a snack
with friends ...

you are being fair.

When you ask other children to
join in …

you are being fair.

When you let other people choose
what to play ...

you are being fair.

When you think about how
other people feel ...

you are being fair.

Being fair is important.

How can you be fair?

Activity

How is this child being fair?

Picture glossary

fair agreeable for everyone

share to let someone else use what you have; to give someone else a part of what you have

Index

Note to Parents and Teachers

Before reading
Ask the children if they have ever heard people say "It's not fair". Explain that being fair means thinking of others and seeing if they can help. Ask them if they have ever said "It's not fair." Why did they think it was unfair? How could they have made things better?

After reading
• Tell the children two puppets have had a quarrel. They have been unkind to each other - perhaps one has taken the other's toy. The other puppet is crying. Ask the children what the puppets should do to be friends again.
• Make up a poem with the class. Ask them to share all the things they like about their friends. The poem could start "Friends are kind and share their toys...". Display the poem for others to read.
• Make a mobile. Ask the children to draw onto thin card something that shows they are being fair. They could use the book for ideas. Cut out the drawings and suspend them from a coat hanger in the classroom.